Barnet Fair, by H. Crane, 1845

BARNET, EDGWARE,
HADLEY AND TOTTERIDGE
A Pictorial History

Boundary House in Barnet High Street as it appeared in *Cowing's Guide to Chipping Barnet and Neighbourhood* in 1887. This was an enlarged second edition of the successful 1876 *Vistors' Handbook to Chipping Barnet*.

BARNET, EDGWARE, HADLEY AND TOTTERIDGE

A Pictorial History

Pamela Taylor and Joanna Corden

Barnet Libraries Arts and Museums

Phillimore

1994

Published by
PHILLIMORE & CO. LTD.
Shopwyke Manor Barn, Chichester, Sussex

ISBN 0 85033 918 9

Printed and bound in Great Britain by
BIDDLES LTD.
Guildford, Surrey

List of Illustrations

Acknowledgements

For the northern part of the borough our debts to others are even greater than usual. The way the boundaries fall ensures co-operation with neighbouring local studies centres, and grateful reliance on local historians interested in different groupings. The strength of the Barnet and District Local History Society made the area's libraries a less obvious focus for local history depositors. The Society's collection, now housed at Barnet Museum, and the local knowledge of its curators both present and past have been a constant support. A full list of acknowledgements would be impossibly long, but we should like to thank especially Graham Dalling, Eric Daw, Jane Downey, Christopher Eve, Andrew Forsyth, Bill Gelder, Gillian Gear, Stewart Gillies, K.Greenwood, Diana Griffith, John Heathfield, A.S. Mays, F.W. Peters, Alf Porter, Sid Ray, Gillian Sheldrick, Maureen Tayler, Bob Thomson and Doreen Willcocks.

More detail and references, as well as further evidence of our debt, will be found especially in H.S. Gieke, 'Notes on the Church and Parish of Edgware' (1957-60, MS in Local Studies Centre), D. Griffith, *Book of Totteridge* (1992), A.S. Jackson, *Semi-Detached London* (1973; second edition 1991), B.R. Leftwich, 'Annals of the Parish and Township of Chipping Barnet' (1950, typescript in Local Studies Centre), P. Taylor (ed.), *A Place in Time* (1989), and the relevant chapters in the *Victoria County Histories*.

Illustration Acknowledgements

The authors wish to thank the following for the use of illustrations: D. Cumplen, 90, 146; Jane Downey, cover photo, 19c, 31, 63, 117, 162; Lesley Eva, 114; Andrew Forsyth, 69, 95, 116, 126; D.W.K. Jones, 158; John Laing Limited, 151; London Borough of Enfield Local History Unit, 103; Northern Telecom Europe Ltd., 129; Charles Russell Solicitors, 7; John Tidmarsh, 119; The Warden and Fellows of All Souls College, Oxford, 15. The rest of the illustrations are from originals and copies in the collections of Barnet Libraries' Archives and Local Studies Centre.

Introduction

This book completes the trilogy covering the area of the London Borough of Barnet. Although it lacks the obvious unity of its predecessors (devoted respectively to Finchley and Friern Barnet, and to Hendon), there are many unifying themes.

One of these is the difficulties of boundaries. The London Borough was created in 1965 by amalgamating several units. Barnet, Edgware, Hadley and Totteridge were all manors and parishes existing by the 11th to 12th centuries, but their historic boundaries divided some settlements and communities. Today the most extreme example is Edgware, where the western boundary of St Margaret Edgware, and the borough, runs along the centre of the Edgware Road. The further side falls to St Lawrence Little Stanmore, and thus to Harrow. The north-western tip of Edgware parish included the south-eastern corner of Elstree village, which was therefore included in the borough in 1965. In 1993, however, the whole of Elstree (previously split three ways) was allocated to Hertsmere, in Hertfordshire.

Chipping Barnet too was divided, roughly along Wood Street, Union Street and the High Street, with the area to the north and west lying in the manor and parish of South Mimms. The relevant parts of Mimms were added when Barnet became a Local Board in 1863. There were further rationalisations involving Barnet, Hadley and Mimms at various times thereafter, most recently in 1993. At the north-eastern corner of the borough, Cockfosters has always been divided, with only a small section lying within Barnet. To make matters worse, largely because of their manorial lordship in the 11th or 12th centuries, Barnet and Totteridge until 1965 lay in Hertfordshire and Edgware and Hadley, together with South Mimms, in Middlesex. The rationalisations have therefore also included transferring land between counties.

Since this book is concerned with the London Borough, we have tried (however regretfully) to keep within its boundaries. Pictures of the Edgware Road are focussed on the eastern side, and most of Cockfosters is missing. We have, though, included parts which were within the borough from 1965 to 1993.

The history of the whole area has been dominated by two factors. One is the heavy clay soil, and the other its position within London's hinterland and on the main routes from London to St Albans and the north. The soil was unattractive to early settlers, and there are relatively few archaeological finds, both before and after London was founded by the Romans. The major exception is Brockley Hill, on the Edgware Road just below Elstree, where pre-Roman field systems have been identified. This was almost certainly the site of Sullionacis, a staging post half-way between London and Verulamium (St Albans). It was also until the second century an important Roman pottery. The kilns exploited both the local clay and the position on a main Roman route. Like almost all the later permanent settlements within our area, with its combination of a heavy soil and high water table, the Brockley Hill activities were sited on high or rising ground.

Both the Edgware Road (which was also a pre-Roman route and whose name of Watling Street is derived from a post-Roman Anglo-Saxon tribe) and the more easterly major Roman road to the north, Ermine Street which passes east of the borough, avoid the Northern Heights. It was not until *c.*1100 that another route was attempted which confronted them, running from Whetstone up to Chipping Barnet and thence to St Albans. The later branch, from Hadley towards Hatfield, gave it the name of the Great North Road. Although Chipping Barnet, on its prominent hill, seems an obvious site, there is no sign of any regular settlement there before the arrival of the road.

There was probably little settlement anywhere on the heavy, densely-wooded soil in the early Anglo-Saxon period. The only place-names which are likely to be early are at Totteridge. Hadley, and probably Barnet, seem to be later names denoting clearings. Edgware is interesting in that Ecgi's weir was presumably on the Deansbrook, but the settlement is up the hill. There were other scattered hamlets, such as Elstree or Arkley, which were probably no less early or important than those which gave their names to the manors and parishes. Again because of the soil, scattered settlement continued, rather than the amalgamation into large villages typical of fully cleared, corn-growing districts.

It used to be thought that most of the settlements might be as late as the 12th century, but very recently (and since *Finchley and Friern Barnet* was written) some new evidence, including a detailed boundary description, has been discovered. This shows that in 1005 King Æthelred granted St Albans Abbey Kingsbury in St Albans, and that with Kingsbury went woodland which corresponds more or less exactly to the later manor of Barnet. The circuit starts at 'hæwenes hlæwe', possibly the earthwork in Hadley Wood, and goes along the Enfield boundary; the next stretch is obscure but after Betstile (New Southgate) the line runs north-west 'along the bishop's boundary', that is between East and Friern Barnet, to Agate, the hill now at the junction of the Great North Road and Northumberland Avenue, and for long the site of the manor mill. It then goes along the edges of Totteridge and Hendon up to Grendels Gate, now Barnet Gate, along the Shenley boundary and by Rowley and Hadley to complete the circuit.

This new evidence is all the more welcome because in the whole of the London Borough of Barnet the only manor separately named and described in the Domesday Book of 1086 is Hendon. All the others are hidden because they were attached, like Barnet in 1005, to other places. Edgware is probably within either Kingsbury (Middlesex) or Stanmore. Hadley was still part of Geoffrey de Mandeville's berewick (farm) of South Mimms. Totteridge may already have belonged to Ely Abbey, in which case it was in 1086, as later, attached to the manor of Hatfield, Herts.

By 1200 the area was rather more obviously on the map: the new road to the north had been built and Chipping Barnet (originally Barnetley) founded. In 1199 it received a market charter—Chipping means market—and must have been developing fast. We have more evidence too of other parts. Geoffrey de Mandeville gave a hermitage at Hadley to Walden Abbey in 1136, and the present 15th-century church (St Mary's) had a 12th-century predecessor. The earliest surviving fabric at another St Mary's, at East Barnet, dates from *c.*1140. St Andrew's at Totteridge (which until the 16th century was dedicated to St Etheldreda, the patron saint of Ely) existed by the 13th century but has been completely rebuilt.

Edgware church existed by the mid-13th century, and in the 12th and 13th centuries there was a chapel near Elstree on some St Bartholomew's Hospital land. The different manorial holdings make Edgware's medieval history highly complicated, but the main manor passed to All Souls College Oxford in 1442. Edgware's potential development as a market seems to have been hindered by Chipping Barnet.

The records and surveys from the various manors supply a lot of detail about the life of the area. There were some common arable fields for a while, but woodland remained a major resource, and many clearances were always for enclosed pasture fields. Although Chipping Barnet functioned as a town it had no manorial independence, and its inhabitants found this increasingly trying even before the Black Death of 1348-9. The death toll—and at its peak deaths of heads of holdings in Barnet rose from the usual one or two per half year to a horrifying 81—altered the balance of power between lords and tenants, and it was the lords' reluctance to admit this which led to the Peasants' Revolt of 1381, in which the men of Barnet were prominent.

Local awareness of the wider world was also increased because of the road. Armies marched to and from London throughout the Wars of the Roses, and as a result two battles were fought at St Albans and one at Barnet. At the Battle of Barnet, fought over Hadley Green on Easter Sunday 1471, the Earl of Warwick, leading the Lancastrians, died and the Yorkists won what proved to be a decisive victory. Places where the Earl is supposed to have fallen are still commemorated, and the Battle of Barnet hedge is old enough for the legend that it sheltered the Lancastrians on the eve of the battle to be possible.

The Wars of the Roses ended with the accession of Henry VII in 1485, and it was his son, Henry VIII, who instituted the Reformation. Although England was spared a further civil war, there were executions at different stages of both Protestant and Catholic martyrs. William Hale, a Protestant, was burnt at the stake in Chipping Barnet in 1555. Henry VIII's dissolution of the monasteries meant that most of the local manors passed into lay ownership, although All Souls, as an educational establishment, was unaffected. Partly to replace monastic provision, a number of new schools were founded and Queen Elizabeth's Boys' (Grammar School), chartered in 1573, was one of these. The original block still survives. So too, at Hadley, does a cottage dating from at least 1521 which is probably the earliest surviving domestic building in the area. The cresset on Hadley church tower may have been used as a beacon in the early warning system which operated in 1588 to signal the approach of the Spanish Armada.

The shake-up of manors hastened the transfer of local government activity from manors to parishes, and in the late 16th century an Act made poor relief—which because of economic change and dislocation was an increasing problem—a parish responsibility. In areas where nucleated villages contained one church but several manors this must have been helpful, but in ours it made far less difference. Down to the 18th century cucking stools and stocks or pillories were provided in Hadley by the parish but in Edgware by the manor. The manors also continued to be important for registering land transfers and regulating commons. Today, only Totteridge Manor remains active, but it has outlasted the others by less than a century.

Underneath the political and religious upheavals, the same underlying factors dominated our local history, and indeed did so until at least the 19th century. As London continued to grow, so did its demand for food and transport. Barnet's market flourished, and in 1588 it was also granted annual fairs. Successful merchants continued to invest in local land, and to consider building country seats in an area which combined sufficient distance with good access to the city. Many of our surviving or recorded 18th-century mansions replaced earlier buildings. The gap between rich and poor was immense and some benefactors helped the parishes as they struggled with poor relief by providing almshouses. Some of these, dating from the 17th century onwards, are among our most attractive local buildings. Barnet Physick Well, a 17th-century discovery, probably failed to survive as a fashionable spa because (like its contemporary at Hampstead) it was too easily reached by the poor.

Another 17th-century development was an alternative road to the north, diverging from the old one in Hadley (at the Highstone) to go across Bentley Heath to Hatfield and thence to York. It was this which became called the Great North Road, with the earlier route usually known as the (London to) Holyhead Road. Below the divide, the road originally passed right in front of Old Fold, but by the mid-1730s it was diverted slightly east, with the original line preserved as a footpath, and in boundaries.

The Agricultural and Industrial Revolutions of the 18th century allowed further leaps in London's population. Even more than before, the fields of this area were dedicated to growing hay to support the capital's huge horse population. This was a crop ideally suited to the local soil, and needing less regular labour than arable, but it required a lot of extra hands at harvest-time. Many of these seasonal labourers were Irish, and the annual influx is noted in many local sources.

Both the growing population and transport improvements led to a great increase in long-distance travel. The main roads were turnpiked, the Edgware Road after a petition in 1711 which claimed that the stretch including Edgware was so damaged by the weight of traffic as to be almost impassable for half the year. By 1760 Edgware too had a cattle fair, though it was not particularly successful. It soon degenerated into a pleasure fair, and even this had stopped before 1810, when a new one was started. This lasted until about 1855, and included cattle, games and races. Barnet Fair too had cattle, horses, and amusements spreading through the streets and across the common, and by the mid-18th century had become a major racing venue, listed alongside Cheltenham and Newmarket. Only the market, which was held along the High Street, had to be (temporarily) abandoned because of the traffic. All the activity created a heyday for the many coaching inns.

The ever-increasing traffic, the need to march troops as speedily as possible to Holyhead en route to Ireland, and advances in technology, meant that around 1800 many stretches of the road were improved. The competition to lessen the gradient of Barnet Hill was won by Thomas Telford and the old route up via Underhill and Hoggy (later Victoria) Lane was replaced in the 1820s by today's causeway. An alternative scheme by McAdam which would have put the road in a cutting through the town, remains an interesting might-have-been. In 1828 Telford also built a new stretch, now the St Albans Road, striking north-west from the top of Barnet High Street to replace the old route through Hadley and South Mimms.

The drive to improve agricultural efficiency meant that open fields and commons were increasingly under threat. In our area open fields had always been rare, and had already been gradually enclosed. There were however great tracts of common, which were important not just to smallholders grazing their few animals but also for pasturing the large numbers involved in the local markets and fairs. Nevertheless, an initial 135 acres of Barnet Common (which originally stretched from Barnet Hill across to Barnet Gate) was enclosed in 1729 by the then lord of the manor, the Duke of Chandos. With the increased pressure from the Napoleonic Wars, the rest succumbed in 1815. The only surviving patch became Ravenscourt Park, which opened in 1883. Grazing could continue in the new fields, but the racecourse had to move east of Barnet Hill, where it was in terminal decline when the station claimed its site in 1871.

Most of Totteridge Common too was enclosed in the 18th century, but attempts to enclose Hadley Green were finally defeated in 1818. Hadley had already been greatly affected by the enclosure of Enfield Chase in 1777. The commoners were awarded some of the land in compensation, resulting in the enlargement of both Hadley and South Mimms parishes. In 1854 Edgware's common, at Edgwarebury, was also enclosed.

The enclosures caused considerable distress, but their impact was as nothing compared to the coming of the railways. The first lines opened in the 1830s, and almost overnight killed long-distance coach travel, and much long-distance droving. Some of the resultant poverty is chronicled in parish records, and the most obvious visual result is the progressive drop in the number of inns. Middle Row, the island triangle of shops in front of St John's Chipping Barnet, and typical of Hertfordshire market towns, was demolished after a fire in 1889.

The local economy did not collapse completely: local carrying continued, and the hay waggons journeyed to London until early this century, stopping for refreshment at inns. Barnet's market and fairs proved resilient. The market was restarted in 1851, on an off-street site. The pleasure fair especially was boosted when the railways brought crowds of visitors, many from London's East End. The merrymaking led the (absentee) lord of the manor to petition the Home Secretary in 1888 for closure, but the Barnet Fair Defence Committee successfully counterpetitioned, pointing out that some 40,000 head of cattle changed hands, and that drovers, dealers and visitors spent large sums locally. The fair, which provides the cockney rhyming slang for hair, still survives, but barely.

In the 1830s, just before the railway era, the town of Barnet began to expand. Tapster and Moxon Streets were laid out on the east, and Union Street, put through in 1837, started the development of the whole area west of the High Street between Wood Street and the (still new) St Albans Road. Until the 1860s this western block remained in South Mimms. Christ Church opened on the Mimms side in 1845, although both it and St Peter's at Arkley (1840) owed more to their benefactors' wishes to provide low church alternatives than to population expansion. After centuries of disputes, St John's finally achieved independence from St Mary East Barnet in 1866.

Rivalry between Anglicans and nonconformists was also significant. The area had a strong nonconformist tradition with dissenters at Totteridge (including the famous preacher Richard Baxter) by the 17th century, and Barnet and Edgware in the 18th. In the early 19th century when educational provision was expanding, nonconformist desire to challenge the previous Anglican monopoly became an important battle ground. Locally, Anglican (usually National) schools were founded in all the parishes, the earliest being Elizabeth Allen's in Wood Street in 1824, and nonconformist (usually British) alternatives included the Puget-endowed Congregational school at Totteridge (1827). School boards, which were secular, were formed for Edgware (with Little Stanmore) in 1875, and East Barnet in 1893. Following the 1902 Education Act, Hertfordshire and Middlesex County Councils became education authorities, as did Hendon Urban District whose responsibility therefore extended after 1931 to Edgware.

There was some increase in the number of cottages, particularly around the former Barnet Common and at Hadley, in the early to mid-19th century. The first major suburban expansion, though, came with the railway. The Great Northern's line to York opened in 1850. Despite a promise to put a station up in the town, the track was built east of the hill so that the station named Barnet (now New Barnet) was a tidy step away. Meadway preserves the line of the connecting footpath, and carriers plied successfully. The GNR bought up the whole of the old Lyonsdown estate, and immediately sold what was not needed to the British Land Company for development. This was the origin of New Barnet, which grew slowly but steadily for the next half-century, at a time when land to its south was still undeveloped. The GNR also built the Great North London Cemetery next to the line at Brunswick Park.

The Midland company's main line through Edgware (and tunnel under Woodcock Hill) opened in 1868, but there was no station. The GNR's suburban line had, however, arrived the previous year, coming overland from Finsbury Park through Finchley and Mill Hill to terminate there. Almost no suburban development ensued, and a plan to extend the line to Watford was abandoned. In 1872 a second branch forked from Finchley through Totteridge (actually Whetstone) up to High Barnet. Once more a promise to bring the station up the hill was broken, and Chipping Barnet's northern expansion was undoubtedly therefore hindered.

A second line to Edgware, coming through Hendon from Golders Green, opened in 1924, but plans for its extension northwards again foundered. Since the new route was better than the earlier one, after both the Edgware and High Barnet branches through Finchley were closed in 1939 for electrification and incorporation into the Northern line via a tunnel to Archway, the Edgware branch did not reopen to passengers beyond Mill Hill East. Goods traffic continued until 1964. The station site has been occupied since 1990 by the Broadwalk shopping centre.

Besides New Barnet, some other suburban development began, if patchily, in the second half of the century. Villas as well as cottages appeared across the former Barnet Common and in Arkley. Even here, though, growth was slow and, as at New Barnet, many streets were not filled by the century's end. Oakleigh Park station, within range of East Barnet, opened in 1873, but only Jackson Road followed, and only in 1889. Trams, unlike trains, finally climbed Barnet Hill in 1907, and the nearby avenues were built. Even trams did not stimulate Edgware, where only Manor Park Crescent and a few isolated villas are Edwardian.

With at least the possibility of suburban intrusion, alternative uses had to be found for some mansions, usually as schools or convents, but large houses in Hadley and Totteridge could still attract wealthy residents. New houses on a similar scale were added, particularly at Totteridge. Some wealthy industrialists were among those who enjoyed the rural seclusion, but improved transport also brought several industries to Barnet, and Charles Wright's factory (too noisy for Clerkenwell) to Edgware.

Churches provided many people's social life, but as the area developed a range of other clubs and activities, including several golf courses, were started. Special national or royal events were always greeted with enormous enthusiasm. Tootell, writing in 1817, gave boredom as a main factor for relaunching Edgware's fair, and described the enormous enthusiasm and hanging of homemade bunting when royalty passed through. Photos from the mid-19th century onwards show huge arches as well as bunting for royal anniversaries.

Boredom was not the only disadvantage. Social gradation ensured that the various classes seldom mixed socially, and the evil reputation of the workhouses among the poor was well deserved. The 1835 Act grouped parishes into Poor Law Unions, each with a workhouse. The Edgware Union workhouse was in fact built just over the border in Hendon. Hadley and Totteridge fell to the Barnet Union, whose workhouse was built in Wellhouse Lane, and given an infirmary wing in 1895. The workhouse itself closed in 1939, but the infirmary continued first as a Public Assistance Hospital and then from 1948 as part of the NHS, changing its name to Barnet General in 1951. Until the coming of the NHS there were no free hospitals outside the workhouse. Public subscription raised the money for the Victoria Hospital, which opened in 1888 and was incorporated within Barnet General in 1950.

The creation of the Unions was the first recognition that parishes could not meet the increasing needs of their inhabitants. The battle to provide more, and non-denominational, local government was however lengthy. The second half of the century saw a complicated patchwork of permissive legislation to establish boards for various purposes. Chipping Barnet acquired a Local Board of Health in 1863, which covered both the Barnet and Mimms sides of the town and also Hadley.

The main pressure for stronger local authorities came because of increasing health risk. New Barnet was developed without proper sanitation, so that the Pymmes Brook carried cholera to East Barnet in the 1860s, but the vestry's attempts to provide adequately for sewage met considerable opposition. The Public Health Act of 1872 finally established Urban and Rural Sanitary Districts for the whole country, with exisiting Local Boards such as Barnet becoming USDs. East Barnet was initially (like Totteridge) within Barnet RSD, but became its own USD in 1875. Hadley was then split between the two USDs. Edgware was part of Edgware (later Hendon) RSD.

Local government was simplified and strengthened by the 1894 Act, which created Urban and Rural Districts. Barnet and East Barnet became UDs, and Barnet UD was enlarged in 1905 and 1914 to take in Arkley and Totteridge respectively. Edgware was transferred from Hendon RD to Hendon UD in 1931. Hendon became a borough in 1932, but Barnet and East Barnet remained UDs until the creation of the London Borough in 1965. East Barnet, the more active, had a housing committee from 1913. It also ran the fire brigade and the sewage farm, whose vegetable produce was successfully sold at Barnet Market until the 1930s.

The First World War was seen as a watershed not simply because of its horror, but also because the 1920s brought such huge change. This was particularly apparent in our area where, during the 1920s and '30s, suburban housing covered most of both Edgware and East Barnet. Fields, farmhouses, mansions and cottages, the ancient buildings along Edgware High Street and the village centre at Cat Hill all vanished.

Two factors combined to cause this transformation. The inner suburbs were now fully developed, so that new housing had to be provided further afield, and railway lines were extended to stimulate the process. This area was particularly affected by the Golders Green to Edgware extension of 1924 and the Finsbury Park to Cockfosters extension, just east of the borough, in 1933. Those parts with the worst transport links—Totteridge, and the northern ends of Barnet and Edgware—had barely been touched by 1939 when the war stopped further building. After the war the Green Belt was imposed to prevent London's further spread, and thus preserved the still surviving farms, fields, and mansions.

The inter-war years saw the development of new services. The councils provided some housing, and also opened parks. There were new schools and chapels. At Edgware a temporary synagogue was opened in 1934 for what was still a small community. Numbers were growing rapidly by the end of the war, and further provision followed. More industry joined Wright's at Edgware, and Standard Telephone and Cables, which moved to New Southgate in 1922, became a major local employer.

Local firms, councils, and of course inhabitants, played a full part in the war effort. Especially since space prevents continuing the story beyond 1945, our final picture stands as a general tribute to them all.

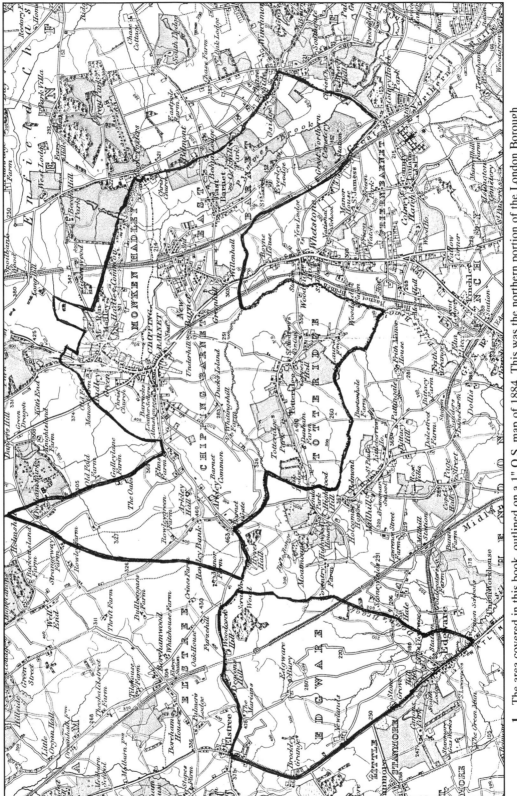

1 The area covered in this book, outlined on a 1" O.S. map of 1884. This was the northern portion of the London Borough from 1965-93. Most of the protruding triangle and the north-west corner at Elstree were then lost, while smaller areas at the eastern base of the triangle and the northern end of Hadley Green were added.

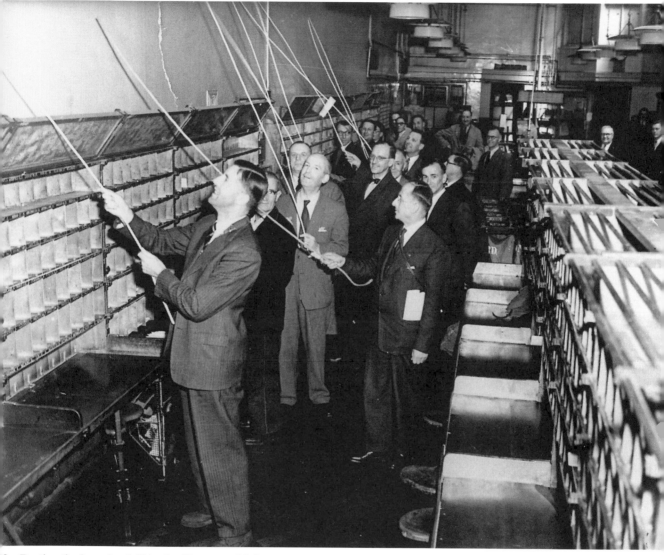

2 Beating the bounds of Chipping Barnet parish in 1957. Parish (and manor) boundaries have changed less than those of later local government units. The fact that the boundary is running through the post office in Barnet High Street explains the need for later changes.

3a & b Brockley Hill is part of Watling Street, the major Roman road from London to St Albans. Pre-Roman fields have been identified here and it was also the site of a major Roman pottery and (probably) the staging post *Sulloniacis*. Archaeologists, including those pictured here in 1951, have made many pottery finds.

4 The *Mitre* yard at the top of Barnet Hill in 1900. Recent excavations have produced 12th- or 13th-century finds but nothing earlier, confirming that this was a new settlement planted on the new Great North Road. The *Mitre* itself, still partly timber-framed, existed by 1633 and had absorbed its neighbours, the *Rose* and *Crown*, by 1667.

5a-e The original parish churches are often the earliest surviving buildings, but all have undergone repeated alteration—as is obvious from these 19th-century prints.

The first pair *(left)*, recorded by Hassell in 1817, are St Mary East Barnet and St Andrew Totteridge. St Mary's still has 12th-century fabric but St Andrew's was completely rebuilt in 1790.

The second pair *(right)*, St Mary Hadley and St John Chipping Barnet, were published by Rock & Co. in 1860 and 1876. St Mary's was rebuilt in 1494 (the date is above the door) and the print shows clearly the cresset or beacon on the tower. St John's was built, probably in the 13th century, as a chapel for the growing town; the print records its alterations, including a major one in 1875.

St Margaret Edgware, in Woodburn's print of 1807 *(left)*, existed in the mid-13th century, but the current tower is 15th-century and the body of the church 18th-19th.

6a There were various settlements at least as old as those which received churches. Elstree (Tidwulf's tree) is mentioned in 10th-century bounds to a purportedly eighth-century charter. Wilson's Cottages, pictured in the foreground *c.*1905, were demolished in the mid-1960s for West View Gardens.

6b Just north of here, Rowley (rough birch clearing) is named in a 1005 boundary. Arkley too has an Anglo-Saxon name, and a history of brick and pottery production going back to at least the 13th century. The cottages in this early 20th-century postcard, though, show 19th-century expansion. The buildings survive but no longer house any post office, shop or tea room.

ARKLEY POST OFFICE

6c The *Old Bell*, now the *Gate*, already has its gate over the inn sign on this *c.*1905 card. Barnet Gate itself, which stands on the parish and county boundary, was for centuries called Grendel's Gate, after the monster in the Anglo-Saxon poem *Beowulf*. Some manor courts were held there, and it may well have been a settlement which shrank as Chipping Barnet grew.

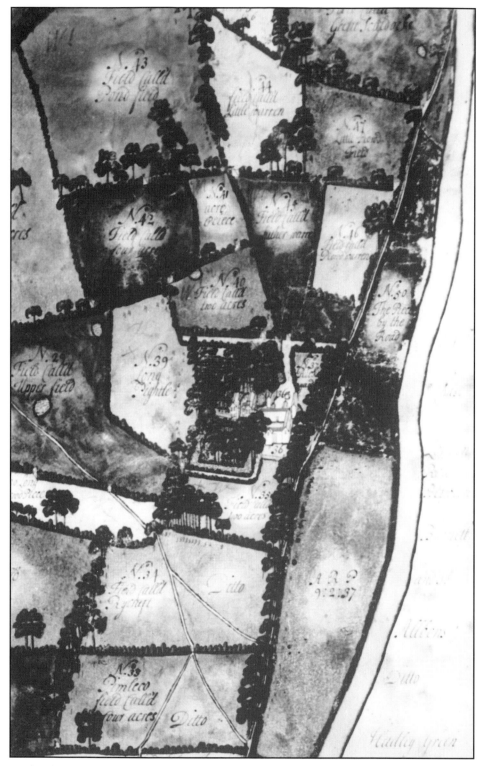

7 Old Fold, west of Hadley Green, was a sub-manor of South Mimms and part of the area transferred to Barnet Local Board in 1863. The manor existed by the 13th century; the earliest part of the current house (since 1910 the golf club house) is 18th-century, but the moat (partly visible in front of the cluster of trees) is medieval. The map was drawn in 1726, and also clearly shows the original line of the Great North Road, preserved as the footpath running between the house and the newer road line.

8 There was no manor house at Edgware but Bury, or Earlsbury, Farm at Edgwarebury acted as the centre, lodging visiting lords of the manor or their representatives. The oldest surviving part of the farm is early 17th-century. The photo shows a hunt leaving the yard in 1946.

9 Edgwarebury Farm, just west of Bury Farm, seems to have been a later neighbour. The 18th-century house, pictured here in 1950, was demolished *c.*1965.

10a & **b**   Two photos of Cat (also Doggetts) Hill. The first, taken *c*.1900, shows the forecourt and corner of the *Cat* inn, which existed by at latest the mid-18th century and burnt down in 1955. The second, slightly later, view looks along the Pymmes Brook to the same cottages. There was already a bridge, called Katebrygge, by 1406. None of the buildings now remain, and the river is under an elongated bridge.

11 Totteridge Lane is a very early route, following a shallow gravel ridge across the clay. Some of its ponds were formed by gravel and clay digging, and heaps of gravel are piled by the roadside in this *c.*1900 photo. Beyond the pond is part of Ellern Mede (then Denham) Farm.

12 Church Hill Road, East Barnet, *c.*1905. As well as connecting the church and Cat Hill, this is part of an early long-distance route and has also been known as East Barnet Lane and Colney Hatch Road. The pond has been drained and the land is now part of Oak Hill Park.

13 The Battle of Barnet was fought over a wide area of Hadley and Barnet in 1471. The Highstone was erected *c*.1740 on the spot where the Earl of Warwick was thought to have fallen, and was shifted slightly north *c*.1840—after this 1805 print. Just visible on the right is a windmill; this was probably fairly recent, and was rebuilt in the 1820s and demolished in the second half of the century.

14 Warwick's Oak by Hadley village, shown here on a *c*.1905 card, marked another supposed sight of the earl's fall. The railings were removed for salvage in 1941 and the tree went soon after. Opposite is the Rectory, built in 1824 by J.R. Thackeray, cousin of the novelist, but rebuilt and divided in the 1950s.

The Old Oak, Hadley Woods

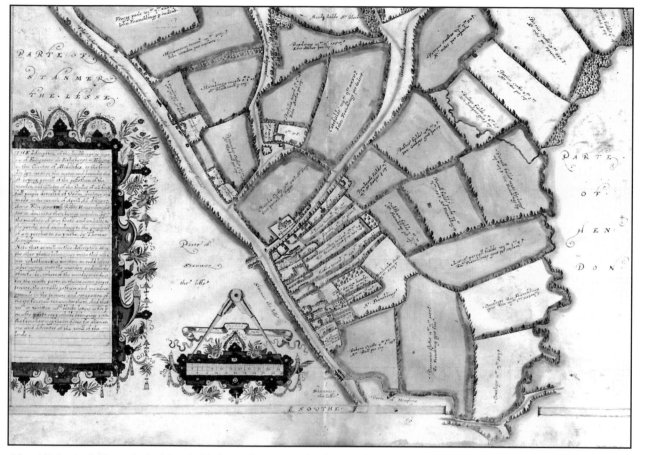

15 All Souls College Oxford has held the main manor of Edgware since 1442, and this wonderfully detailed 1597 map is one of a series describing the estate. The pattern of roads, and of development limited to Watling Street, Church Lane (now Station Road) and Pipers Green, which endured until suburbanisation, was already well established.

16 Purcells, alias Pipers, Farm at Pipers Green, not long before demolition in 1927 to make way for Manor Park Gardens. Purcells tenement is recorded on the previous map. The name Pipers probably comes from the Pypard family, recorded in 1295.

17 This timbered building stood in Church Passage, Barnet, and other versions of the 18th-century drawing show butchers' premises on the front corner. The cross by its side marked the spot where William Hale, a Protestant martyr from Essex, was burnt at the stake in 1555.

18 Latimer's Elm, which stood opposite Hadley Road, was said to be so named because Bishop Hugh Latimer of Worcester, martyred in 1555, once preached under it. In reality it was probably called after a local 17th-century resident, John Latimer. The tree is obviously dying in this card, sent in 1928, and was removed in 1935.

HORSE FAIR BARNET (2)

CATTLE FAIR BARNET (1)

19a-d Barnet's weekly market was chartered in 1199, and its celebrated annual fairs in 1588. Cattle and horses were central to both. The first two cards, from *c.*1905, show the fair animals on the fields near Underhill. The third, from the 1920s, shows the pleasure fair which had long been an important element. The market was driven from the High Street by the stage coaches but then restarted in 1851 on its present St Albans Road site. The fourth card was sent by its auctioneers in 1905. Cattle have now vanished from both, but a horse fair still survives.

20 Middle Row, the island block in front of St John's church, was originally the centre of the weekly market. It was demolished after a bad fire in 1889, not long after this picture was taken.

21 This was Queen Elizabeth's Grammar School, Wood Street, *c.*1920. The towered block is the original one, founded by royal charter in 1573. The school moved in 1932 but the building is preserved as part of Barnet College.

22 Another rare 16th-century survival is this heavily-chimneyed cottage on Hadley Common. It is linked by stairways to its neighbour, Georgian Hurst Cottage. The photograph is from 1952.

23 The Priory at Hadley was never a priory, but a 16th-century building with a sham Gothic stuccoed front added c.1800. Demolished in 1958, it was replaced in 1962 by two neo-Georgian villas. In this c.1915 card Hadley Bourne, built after 1725, can also be seen behind.

24 The Priory at Totteridge, shown beyond the war memorial in 1936. A 17th-century house with 19th-century alterations, it too was never a religious foundation but was renamed in the early 19th century by a relative by marriage of Trollope, Mrs. Garrow, after her grandfather's house, The Priory at Hadley.

25a & b The top picture shows the road junction at the heart of East Barnet village. Beyond Jubilee Terrace (built on Church Hill Road in 1897) lies the Clockhouse, built in the 16th century as Dudmans. It was demolished in 1925, and the replacement Clockhouse Parade, topped by the original clock tower, was barely complete when used as the backdrop for a group outing photo.

26 West Farm (Place) at the north-east tip of Barnet can be traced back to the 17th century, when it belonged to the Norris family. It was rebuilt *c*.1825, and for a while renamed Norrysbury. After about 20 years from *c*.1970-90 as a CEGB training-centre, it was still empty when this picture was taken in 1994.

27 Poynters Grove or Hall, a grand 17th-century mansion, stood north of Totteridge Green. From 1799 until the 1890s it housed the Puget family, whose many local benefactions included the 1827 Congregational chapel and school (now replaced). The Pugets' successor was Geraldine Harmsworth, mother of the newspaper magnates. The etching is one of a series commissioned by her son Cecil, Viscount Rothermere, in 1926. When the house was demolished in 1936 the clock was given to St Andrew's church as a Harmsworth memorial.

28 Church Hill Road early this century, when still-surviving Trevor Lodge was an isolated building. It was the lodge of Trevor Hall, alias Church Hill House, which was designed by Philip Webb in 1860, surrounded by housing in the mid-1930s, and demolished thereafter. Both its names recall an earlier house nearby. This was newly built when it saw Lady Arabella Stuart's detention and escape in 1611, and may have replaced the 16th-century manor house. It later passed to the Trevor family and was demolished in the early 19th century.

29 Sir Roger Wilbrahim built these six almshouses (photographed in 1951) at Hadley in 1612. Hadley was fortunate as another six were endowed by Sir Justinian Pagitt in 1678. The latter were rebuilt in the 19th century. The pattern of 17th-century endowment, often with 19th-century rebuilding, is common, and also applies to Atkinson's at Edgware.

30 Eleanor Palmer endowed the poor of Barnet with land in Kentish Town in 1585, and when its value rose sharply the trustees built these Wood Street almshouses in 1823. Shown here early this century, they were completely rebuilt in 1930.

31 James Ravenscroft, lawyer, merchant, and graduate of Jesus College Cambridge, built his Wood Street almshouses in 1672 and in 1679 established their permanent endowment, as the Jesus Hospital Charity, with land in Barnet and Stepney. The proceeds have allowed more almshouses in Potters Lane (1929 and 1950) and Grasvenor Avenue (1934 and 1950) as well as many grants to the Queen Elizabeth schools and other local charities.

32 Ravenscroft bequeathed more Stepney land, the Chancel estate, to maintain his parents' tomb, the grandest monument in Barnet church. The surplus has covered the 1875 church enlargement, and the building of Bells Hill cemetery in 1895, the attached St Stephen's church in 1896, and St Mark's Barnet Vale in 1899. This interior of St Stephen's comes from an early 20th-century card.

33 Elm Farm alias Three Elms Farm survived the lightning strike and still stands at the foot of Galley Lane. The adjacent barn was built, possibly of local bricks, in 1625. It has now been converted into housing.

Oak Tree struck by Lightning, Sept. 10th, 1869, at Elm Farm, Barnet Common.

BUCHANAN. PHOTO.

34 Totteridge tithe barn, seen beyond the ancient yew tree in the churchyard *c*.1900. Totteridge has three surviving weatherboarded and probably 17th-century barns but both the others, at Laurel Farm and West End House, have been converted into houses.

35 Another surviving 17th- or 18th-century barn is at Stonegrove. Currently a garden centre, it is shown here *c*.1904, with accompanying hay carts, when it was still part of Nicolls Farm. The adjacent farmhouse became empty *c*.1960 and was demolished thereafter.

36 Dr. Trinder (of Trinders Lodge, Arkley) was trying, unsuccessfully, in 1812 to revive use of the Barnet Physick Well. Discovered in 1652, it had a brief vogue and was visited by Pepys. Both then and in 1812 it was too accessible to remain fashionable, and has been unused since the mid-19th century. The present wellhouse was built in 1937.

37 William Stevens, draper's and tailor's of Barnet High Street, adorned for the coronation of Edward VII in 1902. From the 16th century this was the inn called the *Lion* or *Red Lion*, and it was here that Pepys stayed in 1667. In the 18th century it was converted to Assembly Rooms, and thereafter to a theatre. The narrow entry to Tapster Street, laid out in the 1830s, probably uses the old entry to the inn yard.

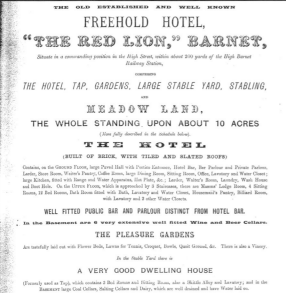

38 This *Red Lion* took over the name when the other one closed. Previously the *Antelope* and *Cardinals Hat*, it was one of Barnet's oldest and largest inns. When this 1890 sale catalogue was made it was still intact, but within 20 years Fitzjohns Avenue was cut through both inn and grounds. The still imposing replacement is now called *The Dandy Lion*.

39 Barnet Fair fostered many fringe amusements, as these extracts from a *c.*1756 racing guide show. The racecourse was on Barnet Common but moved eastward at the latter's enclosure. The races declined thereafter and finished in 1870, with two walkovers and one race with three horses, just before the new railway line was built across the site.

HERTFORDSHIRE.

The Cock Match fought at *Barnet*, on the 27th of *July* and following Days, being the Time of the Races, was a Drawn Main.

AUGUST, 1756.

BARNET——HERTFORDSHIRE.

ON the 3d of *August*, 50 *l.* was run for, by such as never won more Plates than one of that Value, free for any other Horse, &c. that had not won 40 *l.* from the first of *March* to the Day of Starting for this Plate, 4 Year Olds, Wt. 7 ft. 5 Year Olds 8 ft. 6 Year Olds 9 ft. and full aged 9 ft. 10 lb. Horses, &c. that never won 40 *l.* at one Time to be allowed 5 lb. This Prize was won by

	H. 1	H. 2	H. 3
Mr. *Swymmer's* Br. H. *Mirza*, aged —	2	1	1
Mr. *Rebow's* Bay M. *Rose*, aged ———	1	4	4
Capt. *Vernon's* Gr. H. *Beau*, 6 Years old	3	2	2
Mr. *Burfoot's* Bay M. *Louisa*, 6 Years old	4	3	3
Mr. *Jennison's* Bay H. *Ruffler*, 5 Years old	5	dif	
Ld. *Chedworth's* Br. H. *Bauble*, 5 Years old, distanced by a Person riding against him and throwing him down	dif		

On the 4th, 50 *l.* was run for, by such as never won more Plates than one of that Value, free for any other Horse, &c. that had not won 50 *l.* from the first of *March* to the Day of Starting for this Plate, 14 Hands, 4 Year Olds, Wt. 7 ft. 11 lb. 5 Year Olds 8 ft. 7 lb. 6 Year Olds 9 ft. and full aged 9 ft. 7 lb. Give and Take, which Prize was won by

	H. 1	H. 2	H. 3
Mr. *Boothby's* Chef. H. *Grantham*, 6 Years old, 14 H. 1/4 th, Wt. 9 ft. 1 lb. 12 oz.	1	5	1
Mr. *Chamberlane's* Bay H. *Ruby*, 6 Years old, 14 H. 2 I. 3/8 ths, Wt. 10 ft. 2 lb. 10 oz.	4	1	2
E 3			Ld.

The Old Stocks,
Hadley Green.

40 Hadley in the 17th and 18th centuries had a whipping post and cucking stool as well as stocks—which were rebuilt in 1787 and 1827. These survivors, shown on a *c*.1908 postcard, stood on the green until 1935 when they were accidentally destroyed by the celebration bonfire for George V's jubilee.

41 Hadley Green, Pond and Brewery *c.*1910. The brewery was established by 1770. It was rebuilt in 1911 and continued to brew until acquired in 1938 by Fremlins, who made it a distribution centre. In 1967 Whitbread took over, and closed it in 1969. The site was bought by Crest Homes in 1977 and the brewery was demolished the next year.

42 The elegant row of 18th-century houses still lines the east side of Hadley Green, as it did when this early 20th-century postcard was made. Livingstone Cottage is on the extreme left, lived in by the explorer and his family for nine months in 1857. Next comes Monken Cottage, then Monkenholt, Fairholt and Hadley House.

43 This 1947 photo shows Hadley Hurst, bordering the Common, reputedly designed by Wren and certainly built before 1707: a fine mansion with magnificent cedar trees on the lawn. In 1936 its owner Gordon Saunders (who at other times also lived at Monkenholt and The Chase) sold the Council what became King George V Field for public enjoyment in perpetuity. A footpath to it passes the house.

44 Another photo of similar date showing Mount House, Camlet Way, a perfect example of an 18th-century villa. It was built on rising land enclosed from Enfield Chase, and remained within Enfield until 1882. In 1947 the Sisters of St Martha moved the senior wing of their school here from Wood Street, and in 1949 bought Hadley Bourne in Dury Road to accommodate their boarders.

45 Totteridge Manor House was built for the Lee family soon after they acquired the lordship of the manor in the mid-18th century. The photograph was taken *c.*1900.

46 On a larger scale is Totteridge Park, the main Lee family residence from the mid-18th century to the early 19th, and now Totteridge's only surviving grand mansion. From 1851-94 it was a nonconformist boarding school, and this photo of the early 18th-century east front was found bound with school magazines. Thereafter, unusually, it reverted for a time to private ownership. It is now flats.

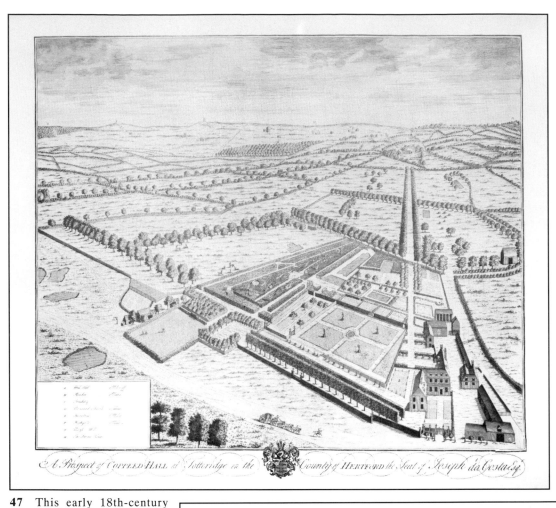

A Prospect of Copped Hall at Totteridge in the County of Hertford the Seat of Joseph da Costa Esq.

47 This early 18th-century print of Copped Hall captures the scale of such estates. First mentioned in the 16th century, it was demolished in 1928 by its owner, George Kemp the biscuit magnate. Most of the grounds (less formally relandscaped by Repton) became Darlands Nature Reserve in 1971. Among famous owners were the Mannings (the Cardinal was born here) and from 1862-8 Lord (Bulwer) Lytton who, because of his Wars of the Roses novel, is commemorated in New Barnet street names.

48 Littlegrove was rebuilt in 1719 as New Place, but the old name soon reappeared. Even this was a replacement of the medieval Danegrove. The house was the childhood home of F.C. Cass, the local historian. It was much enlarged in the 19th century and demolished in 1932, although some of the garden wall remains.

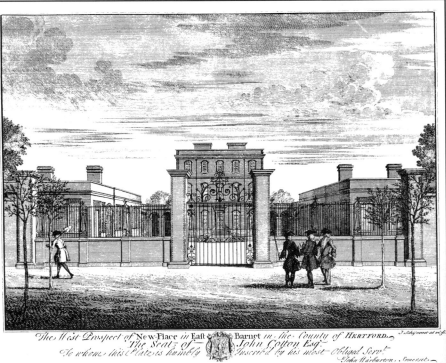

The West Prospect of New-Place in East Barnet in the County of Hertford. The Seat of — John Cotton Esq. To whom this Plate is humbly Inscrib'd by his most Obliged Serv.t John Warburton. Somerset.

49a & b Oakhill Theological College (above) still dominates the view across the park that bears its name. The house was built *c*.1790 within the grounds of Monk(en)frith House (below), which existed by the 17th century and was demolished in 1937. This name, meaning monks' wood, was used for the area from the Middle Ages until gradually replaced by Oakhill. The last private owner of Oakhill, Charles Baring Young, died in 1928 leaving it to be used with Bohun Lodge (the latter in fact only until 1937) as a theological college.

50a & **b** Greenhill and Willenhall were originally one large estate known, like the stretch of the Great North Road on which it lay, as Pricklers (from the medieval Pritel family). By the 16th century it was called Greenhill. It was split in 1820 when Thomas Wyatt built Willenhall on the southern part; this was demolished for development around 1900. Greenhill almost became a public park in 1926, but after public resistance most was sold for building. The photos show two survivals: above, the arches on Willenhall Avenue, reduced to mere pillars since this *c.*1930 picture was taken; below, Greenhill lake, seen here in the 1928 sale catalogue.

51 The Hill House at Elstree is a fine 18th-century building with 18th- and 19th-century additions: some of the range can be seen in this 1950 view of the back. Elstree School started here in 1847, but apparently replaced an earlier foundation. It moved in 1939 and after a brief time as a teacher training college, the house has provided sheltered accommodation since 1949.

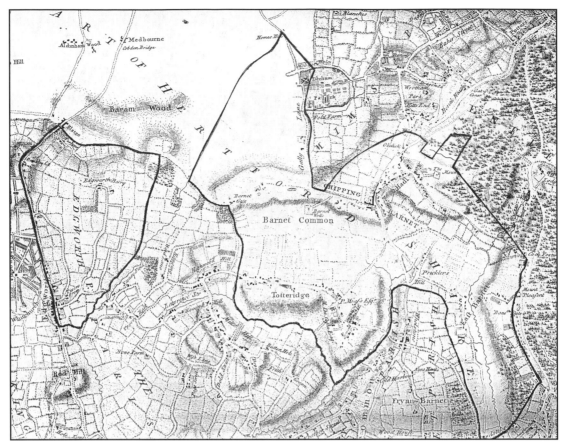

52 Rocque's 1754 map is of Middlesex but luckily includes something on most of our area (boundaries are added). One obvious feature is the expanse of still unenclosed Barnet Common. Below in Totteridge he notes only the estates of Messrs. Mias (*recte* Meyer, at Poynters) and Da Costa (Copped Hall). Although usually reliable, his survey of Edgware is inaccurate.

53 When Enfield Chase was enclosed in 1777, 190 acres of common were established in Hadley, of which Hadley Woods are the eastern part. They are as popular now as they were in Victorian and Edwardian times, although sadly donkey rides are no longer available.

54 Barnet and Hadley had famous nursery gardens from the 18th century, but William Cutbush did not arrive in the area until *c.*1840. The nursery (commemorated in Nursery Row) was still flourishing in 1932, the date of this advertisement, but in 1937 the St Albans Road site closed, to become a drill hall.

55 Arkley mill was built in 1806 and remained in use until the First World War, although latterly, as this Edwardian card shows, with only one pair of sails. Since then it has been restored several times, and is still visible within the grounds of Windmill House (built 1929).

56 An attractive 1805 print of Barnet High Street. The cart is turning into what was long known as The Squeeze, while the lame pedestrian is heading towards Church Passage. Of the buildings shown, only the church survives.

57 John James Cowing established his print, book and stationer's shop in Barnet High Street in 1805, and two of his sons founded the *Barnet Press* there in 1859. The shop front, pictured early this century, was a local feature for many years. The premises were vacated in 1986. As well as the newspaper, postcards and guides produced by Cowings are an abiding local history source.

58 The Whalebones gateway in Wood Street. The fashion for these was long-lived and widespread, and there is another pair at Totteridge. This set, shown here *c*.1910, was probably erected *c*.1875. The bones had to be replaced in 1939, soon after the house was bought by Miss Gwynneth Cowing.

59a & **b** The Day almshouses at Stonegrove were founded in 1828 by Charles Day, a local resident and partner in Day and Martin's successful boot-blacking firm. One of the houses burnt down and was rebuilt c.1886 and all were restored in 1959. The top card shows them c.1915. The other card shows Blacking Bottle Lodge, shaped like the source of Day's fortune, which stood at the entrance to his mansion, Edgware Place.

60 The original road to St Albans and the north went from Barnet via Hadley and South Mimms. The stretch shown here *c.*1930, the New or St Albans Road, was put through in 1828 (greatly diminishing the *Green Man*'s grounds) as part of the major improvements to what was by then known as the London to Holyhead road.

61 This 1920s view south to Underhill shows the *Old Red Lion* (a small inn since the 18th century, not to be confused with the larger establishments up the hill) and Underhill, or Sharp's, Farm. The cottages between (demolished 1934-5 fairly soon after this card was made) mark the foot of the old route up the hill, which was replaced in the 1820s improvements by the causeway to the east.

62 The junction of Union Street and Barnet High Street, sketched by a local artist. Union Street was laid out in 1837, opening up development west of the High Street. It was cut through the southern part of another of the town's large inns, the *Hartshorns*. The inn itself went in 1929 but the smaller *Star Tavern*, seen opposite, survived until 1959.

63 Sandwiched between *The Old Windmill* (there by 1752) and *The Two Brewers* (by 1803), the name of *The King William IV* at Hadley Highstone probably gives the date of its opening. It was taken over by the Canon Brewery in 1927. *The Two Brewers* was demolished in 1992.

64 Although Elizabeth Allen left money in 1727 to build a free school in Barnet, until 1823 it was used to support Queen Elizabeth's. It was then reclaimed to help build the Elizabeth Allen Parochial Schools, which opened in Wood Street in 1824. Seen here in a later 19th-century print, the school closed in 1973 but the buildings remain.

65 Moxon Street (named after its builder) was laid out east of Barnet High Street in the 1830s and this British, ie. Nonconformist, School opened soon afterwards. The building is charming but obviously constricted, and closed as a school in 1933, more or less when this photo was taken.

66 Children outside St Andrew's School on Totteridge Green, *c*.1905. The school was founded in 1837 and rebuilt in 1939. Beyond is the *Orange Tree*, in existence by 1668 but much rebuilt. Its pond, just visible beyond the trees, still encourages ducks and geese to the common.

67 A concert party from Christ Church Boys' School, *c*.1910. Christ Church opened in 1845 and, being on Mimms Side, was initially a chapel of St Giles, South Mimms. The Pennefather Hall, seen in the background, opened in 1907. The school opened next to the church site in 1844 and the Alston Road buildings, for long the boys' school, followed in 1880. The whole school came to Alston Road in 1952. The infants moved to Byng Road in 1962 and the juniors followed in 1968.

68 East Barnet National (Church of England) School as it looked *c*.1906. It was built in 1872 (with much of the money provided by Mr Thornton, commemorated in nearby Thornton Road) and replaced other premises. It chose not to come under the new East Barnet School Board in 1893. Now called St Mary's, it still retains its village atmosphere.

69 The Leathersellers' Almshouses were built off Union Street between *c.*1838 and 1866, in striking Gothic style, for the 'aged poor' of the City Company. Shown here in the 1930s, they were largely rebuilt in 1964-6.

70 Edgwarebury Lane, seen in the 1920s before housing transformed all but the northern end. The northern stretch, now partly a footpath, was diverted eastwards when Edgwarebury Common was enclosed in 1854. Until then it joined the now truncated Fortune Lane.

71 From 1840 Barnet and Edgware came within the Metropolitan Police district. A policeman is standing in the doorway of the Barnet station in this early 20th-century card. This 1860s building was replaced in 1915 by a new one next door, for which Jacksons Forge and its northern neighbours were demolished in 1909. The station was again rebuilt in 1974.

72 The Pymmes Brook has a history of intermittent flooding which, when housing increased without proper drainage, added to its potential as a health hazard. On this occasion, in April 1878, an early photographer was on hand.

73 The Great Northern's main line and station opened in 1850 on flat land well east of High Barnet. The company bought the whole Lyonsdown estate and sold the rest for development, making New Barnet a 19th- rather than a 20th-century suburb. This photo along The Triangle was taken shortly before the original station was demolished in 1894 during track widening.

74 The junction of Lyonsdown Road and Long Street, *c*.1905. Lyonsdown Road was one of the first to be put through in creating New Barnet. Long Street, the far earlier route to East Barnet, was renamed Longmore Avenue in 1931 when both roads were modernised. Their shared course until the junction loops round Greenhill Park, seen on the left.

75 Because of the Battle of Barnet, many street names in New Barnet were derived from the Wars of the Roses. This postcard of Leicester Road looking west from the junction with Plantaganet Road was sent in 1906, when cars were probably a more unusual sight than sheep.

76 Nos.1-14 Warwick Cottages were among the earlier and cheaper developments in New Barnet, predating *The Warwick* inn on the corner. Seen here *c*.1955, the cottages and cul-de-sac were replaced in the early 1960s by Warwick Close.

The advent of the Motor Hearse has made this Cemetery easily accessible from all parts of London, enabling dwellers in this overcrowded and huge city to select a burying place still unmarred by serried rows of monuments, wherein the dead may rest in dignity and peace amid beautiful and natural surroundings.

Further particulars can be obtained on application to the Superintendent at New Southgate and private grave sites can be selected, the prices of which compare most favourably with those of other London Cemeteries.

For Motor Routes see Map on next page.

77 By the time of this 1920s brochure, funerals reached the Great Northern Cemetery on Brunswick Park Road by car. When it opened in 1861, though, there was a special siding off the rail line from King's Cross. This part of the scheme was short-lived, but the splendid landscaping and monuments remain.

78   Church Farm lies next to St Mary's church at East Barnet. In 1860 it became a Boys' Home, an industrial school for orphans of good character, specialising in farm training. This photo was taken in 1934 when it had just become an approved school, which moved to Surrey in 1937.

79   The triumphal arch at Hadley to celebrate the Prince of Wales' marriage in 1863 was designed by Mrs. G.W. Millen and executed by the voluntary efforts of Hadley residents. There are photos of a similar arch at Arkley in 1897 for Queen Victoria's Diamond Jubilee.

80 A family photo of Dredge's cooperage at the top of Barnet Hill, taken in 1864-5. The gabled building beyond and its southern neighbour later became classrooms for Queen Elizabeth's Girls' School.

81 Manor Road was one of the first to be laid out between Wood Street and Mays Lane across the former Barnet Common. There was a development company by 1867 but building remained obstinately slow until the turn of the century. By the time this card was sent in 1912 it was fairly complete.

82 Barnet Methodist chapel, at the Hadley end of the High Street, soon after it was enlarged in 1871. The 1839 building replaced two cottages used for worship since 1760, where John Wesley had preached. The Methodists moved slightly south in 1891 (to the chapel whose front has since 1989 been incorporated into the Spires shopping centre) and this building was sold to the Baptists.

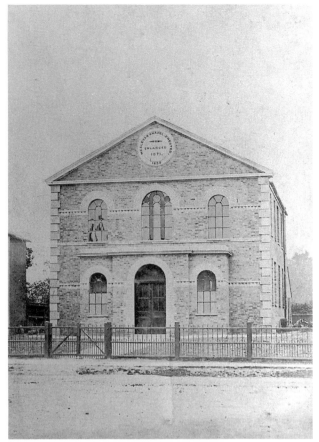

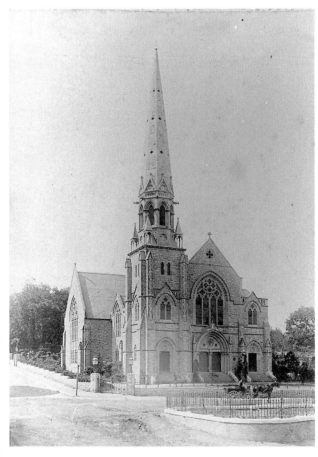

83 The imposing New Barnet Methodist chapel opened on the corner of Station and Lyonsdown Roads in 1880, replacing temporary premises elsewhere. A number of other nonconformist chapels were opening in the area at this time (see plate 84). Like many of the others, this one's scale became inappropriate, and it was demolished in 1963.

84 Station Road New Barnet looking west about 1912, and encapsulating much of the area's development. In front is East Barnet Town Hall, built for the Local Board in 1892 and today boarded up. Beyond can be seen the pediment of the Baptist chapel (1872-1982) and the spire of the Congregational church (1880-1967).

85 The society, which still flourishes, began in 1874 as the New Barnet Young Men's Mutual Improvement Society. Women were admitted from 1880, although for some years they were not allowed to speak. The Eisteddfod was held in 1900 at the Assembly Rooms in Lytton Road where in 1895 Birt Acres gave one of his first moving picture shows. The rooms were replaced by a cinema in 1926. (See also plates 105 and 138.)

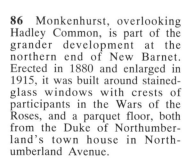

86 Monkenhurst, overlooking Hadley Common, is part of the grander development at the northern end of New Barnet. Erected in 1880 and enlarged in 1915, it was built around stained-glass windows with crests of participants in the Wars of the Roses, and a parquet floor, both from the Duke of Northumberland's town house in Northumberland Avenue.

HIGH BARNET STATION.

87 High Barnet station opened in 1872, a terminus of a suburban line. Once again, despite the railway company's promises the line failed to climb the hill. There are obvious changes, but this early 20th-century photo is still very recognisable.

Chapel of
St Mary of Nazareth at
Edgware

88 The Anglican Convent of St Mary of the Cross (until 1931 St Mary of Nazareth) and its attached hospital were founded in Shoreditch in 1865. Land north of Hale Lane, Edgware, was bought in 1873, and the whole operation gradually moved there, where it remains. Of the chapel seen here only the Lady Chapel (immediately behind the figures) was built—being blessed in 1891.

89 St Edward's on Totteridge Lane, shown *c.*1905, was opened as a Roman Catholic orphanage by Cardinal Manning in 1875, and later became a boarding school. Since 1958 it has belonged to the White Fathers, a missionary teaching order.

90 There was an estate called Ludgrove at the eastern edge of Hadley by the 15th century, but the house called Ludgrove, seen *c.*1880, is a 19th-century rebuilding of a different mansion (the Blue House). A school from 1890-1937, it was bought for development in 1939, but the war intervened and since compulsory purchase in 1950 it has been used for educational purposes.

91a & b Two late 19th-century pictures which capture the creation of Ravenscroft Park (named after James Ravenscroft, see plates 31 and 32). In 1880 Thomas Smith, the developer of the adjacent housing, offered to pay for converting the last remnant of Barnet Common, near *The Black Horse* in Wood Street, into a park. It opened in 1883 and was extended to include the area shown in both these pictures in 1885. There were once two ponds but since 1992 neither remains.

92 The view north towards Hadley from Barnet High Street at the New Road junction, *c*.1880. The Corn Exchange on the left, in fact the premises of one firm of corn dealers, was replaced by today's building in 1891.

93 An early photo of Queen Elizabeth's Girls' School, which opened in 1888 as an extension of the Tudor boys' foundation. The start was so shaky that in 1895 it nearly closed, but since then it has always flourished.

94 Victoria Cottage Hospital, founded by voluntary contribution, opened on Barnet Hill in 1888 as a memorial to the Queen's 1887 jubilee. It moved to Wood Street in 1923 and was incorporated into Barnet General Hospital in 1950. The original site, seen here *c*.1905, was absorbed into the neighbouring Queen Elizabeth's Girls' School.

VICTORIA COTTAGE HOSPITAL HIGH BARNET

95 Jackson Road, laid out in 1889 and shown *c.*1915, was East Barnet's first suburban development, linking the village towards Oakleigh Park station. William Jackson, the road's builder, later followed his father as licensee of the *Prince of Wales*, and was also a major local benefactor, particularly to Methodism and to Barnet Hospital.

96 Kitts End Road, Hadley, was the third site for a children's nursing home founded by Katherine Pawling in 1890. Purpose-built on land provided by the Earl of Strafford, it was designed by Evelyn Simmonds and officially opened in 1911. This card was sent in 1914. The children's home closed from lack of demand in 1961 but has since reopened as a home for the elderly.

97 The view south down Edgware High Street, *c.*1890. The *George* inn in the foreground existed as part of the George Farm (one of the manorial demesne farms) by 1454, and manor courts were often held there. An Ascension Day fair was held in its yard and adjoining field during the 18th century. This whole row was demolished for road widening *c.*1931.

98a & **b** For centuries until about the First World War, hay and its transport were vital to the local economy, and the mainstay of many inns. Both these photos were taken on the Edgware Road in 1891. The empty carts stand outside *The Leather Bottle*, recorded in the 1750s but then apparently silenced for some time. It was rebuilt *c.*1910 and again in 1931. The full carts are outside *The Boot*, another 18th-century inn whose adjoining stables were of 16th/17th-century timber construction.

99 Another view of *The Boot*, *c.*1900 and showing the usual poor road surface. This was improved when tram tracks were laid in 1904 to a terminus just north of the inn. At the same time the entry to Station Road (then Church Lane) was modernised and the parish pump, seen here beyond the pillar and railings, removed. *The Boot* was rebuilt *c.*1930 and demolished in 1965.

100 A haycart during a refreshment break around the turn of the century. The inn is *The Railway Bell*, close to New Barnet station, emphasising the point that it was cars rather than trains which destroyed local carting.

101a & b There has been an inn at the junction of Wood Street and Galley (previously Gallows) Lane since the 18th century. The top photo shows it in *c.*1890 when (like the farm glimpsed beyond) it was called *The (Three) Elms.* Some 20 years on, when the carriage was pictured outside the stables, it had become the *Arkley Hotel.* Today, rebuilt, it is *The Arkley.*

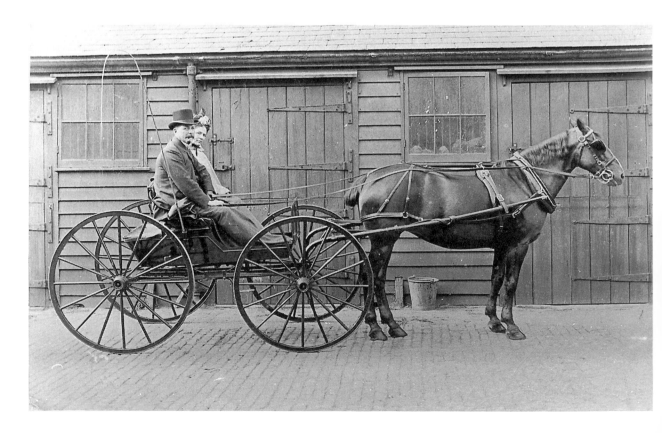

102 The junction of Bells Hill and West End Lane *c.*1900. *The Lord Nelson* (with adjacent cottages called Trafalgar Place) was built in the early 19th century but has been rebuilt. Silesia College, a private school, was in existence by 1878 and lasted into the new century. By 1911 it had become a private house, Oakmede, which was destroyed by a mine in 1940.

103 Sir Thomas Lipton's tree house in the grounds of Osidge House, taken at the turn of the century. The house, an 1808 rebuilding, was sold to Sir Thomas in 1893, the year before he acquired his tea estates in Ceylon. The five-times challenger of the America Cup died in 1931, leaving his entire estate for the relief of Glasgow's poor apart from Osidge, which is now a nurses' home.

104 Barnet Alston FC started as a works team from the Alston Road dental factory which opened in 1891. In 1911 it merged with Barnet Avenue, founded in 1888, to become Barnet and Alston until 1914 and Barnet thereafter. The club turned professional in 1965.

PREFACE.

THE BARNET BOOK OF PHOTO-GRAPHY.

The purpose of this book is to place in the hands of every Photographer instructive articles on essential processes and manipulations, by eminent writers who have given such subjects their especial study, and who have borne in mind that whilst the experienced Amateur and the Professional may each find much to learn from a comparatively elementary description of methods and means, it is the Beginner who stands in greatest need of help.

In the mind of every photographer the name of Barnet is inseparable from a great Photographic Industry, and now it is intended that the name shall be associated with a good and useful book, which is called the BARNET BOOK OF PHOTOGRAPHY, and it is left to the reader to say if the fulfilment of its purpose and the manner of its doing are such as to justify its existence.

To all who are interested in photography, who love it for itself and for its productions, and who desire to improve their own practice of its many processes and applications, this Book is respectfully dedicated.

Barnet, Herts.
April, 1898.

ELLIOTT & SON.

105 Barnet's 'great Photographic Industry' was very much due to Elliott and Son, who had established their photographic printing works at Talbot House in Park Road c.1890. In 1892 Elliott recruited Birt Acres who in 1895 shot Britain's first moving picture, showing his assistant leaving adjacent Clovelly Cottage.

106 Charles Wright brought the first industry to Edgware, moving in 1900 from Clerkenwell to a site behind Edgware and Station Roads, which he developed as Forum Way. Products included medals, advertising signs, number-plates and, during the Second World War, parts for respirator filters. The photo is from a series made in the 1930s and the firm remained in Edgware until 1972.

107 This is one of a trio of houses, including his own, The Croft, built by T.E. Collcutt on Totteridge Green in the 1890s. This one, seen here *c.*1905, has since 1968 housed the Consolata Missionary College.

108 The Grange was the largest house in Totteridge, listed with 27 hearths in the tax of 1663. It was rebuilt in the 18th century, when it belonged to the Lee family, but burnt down in 1899. The replacement, built on the foundations and modelled on its predecessor, was designed by Charles Nicholson, son, and later heir, of the owner. It was turned into flats, Grange Mansions, in 1933.

109 The Leys at Barnet Lane Elstree was built in 1901 for J.B.B. Wellington, a noted innovator and industrialist. He himself took this photo of the hall in its pristine glory in 1903. The house was bought by Middlesex County Council in 1947 to become an old people's home. Since 1980 it has been a Barnet Social Services hostel, although since 1994 it is outside the borough.

110 The north end of Hadley Green *c*.1900, with Old Fold Lane to the left, *The Old Windmill* inn sign on the right, and the cottages at Highstone beyond. Note the children in the perambulators and on the logs by the roadside.

111 The centre of Totteridge village *c*.1905, with two shops and no traffic other than a haycart. There are now cars but no shops: the bay-fronted post office and general store reverted to a private house in the 1970s.

112a & b From 1903-91 East Barnet's fire station was at the junction of Lytton and Leicester Roads. Until a motor engine was bought in 1919, the horses were supplied by a nearby cartage contractor, and the top picture shows his premises. Even proximity did not save Lockhart's sawmills in Leicester Road, shown after they burnt down in 1907.

113 The New Barnet force outside the police station at the junction of Edward and Margaret Roads around the turn of the century. The station opened in 1884, closed in 1933, and was demolished in 1985.

114 Julia Hyde bequeathed £10,000 in 1888 for a literary institute and reading rooms for Chipping Barnet and Hadley. With a further donation from the Misses Paget, the purpose-built premises in Church Passage, with a free reading room and subscription library, opened in 1904. A free county library branch opened in 1925, and the two were merged in the Institute premises in 1929. The library moved to new premises in Stapylton Road in 1991.

Barnet University Extension & Technical Instruction Society.

Technical Exhibition. Session 1900=1.

Certificate, *Second,*

Awarded to *Miss Byfield,*

For *Laundry — Getting up a Muslin Blouse*

Catherine H. Shore Judge.

J. B. Lee M.A. President.

April 24th, 1901.

115 The talents of Dora Byfield, the energetic daughter of East Barnet Council's Clerk, were expended on a range of local organisations and activities. The high-sounding title of this society is belied by the subject.

116 The tram route was extended from Whetstone to the top of Barnet Hill in 1907. This was one of the pictures taken at the new terminus on the opening day, Good Friday, 29 March.

117 Soon after trams, unlike trains, had managed to climb Barnet Hill, Fitzjohn Avenue and its neighbours were laid out for suburban development. Fitzjohn Avenue was cut through the *Red Lion* (now *The Dandy Lion*), halving its frontage.

118 The special car is examining the terminus of the tramline extension from Edgware to Stanmore Corner, which opened on 31 October. The westward road to Stanmore was given by the Duke of Chandos *c.*1717 when he turned the original one into a private avenue through Canons Park. Spur Road, completing today's crossroad, was built with the Edgware Way *c.*1927.

119 H.E. Tidmarsh in his Marriott Road, Barnet studio *c.*1908. Best known for his London street scenes, Tidmarsh also painted and photographed locally and was active in local affairs, especially the promotion of Methodism and Temperance.

120 Manor Park Crescent, with Chilton and Manns Roads, was one of the few Edwardian developments in Edgware (whose 1867 suburban station had notably failed to stimulate building). The roads were laid out on the site of Manor Farm, and Manor Park Crescent absorbed the southern end of Pipers Green Lane.

121 This postcard of the way across the Hale Fields was sent in 1908. The Hale, including the inn (currently *Everglades*), lies just beyond the Deans Brook in Mill Hill.

The Hale Fields, leading from Edgware to the Green Man. Reeves' Series. 188

122 The Rowley Green entrance to Arkley Golf Club, around the time of its opening in 1909. It is almost within striking distance of its near contemporaries, Old Fold Manor (1910) and the South Hertfordshire course at Totteridge (1899).

123 An early car approaching the New Road junction with Barnet High Street. The card was sent in 1913. Opposite *The Wellington* is the small market at Mary Payne's Place.

124 Barnet Brewery in Wood Street had an intermittent existence from at least the 18th century until final closure in 1909, not long after this picture was taken. Council offices opened on the site in 1912. Barnet College for girls was another of the area's private schools, and had gone by 1911. Since 1938 the building has housed Barnet Museum.

Old Court House Park Barnet.

B. & S. Series. 101.

125   Barnet UDC bought the freehold of the Old Court House estate in 1923, and the recreation ground was opened the next year. The Council had been using the building since the new Court House on the corner of Normandy Avenue was built in 1916.

126   Ewen Hall in Wood Street was one of the many buildings that became temporary hospitals in the First World War, and the card shows beds outside. The adjacent Congregational church had built the hall in 1907. The church itself opened in 1893, replacing one of 1824. This had replaced a dissenting chapel of 1719, part of whose graveyard can still be seen from Union Street.

EWEN HALL HOSPITAL, BARNET.

127a & **b** Until 1939 the Frusher family used Folly Farm on the edge of Hadley Woods to fatten pigs in winter, but in summer opened it as a pleasure resort. It was also used for public gatherings, especially during the First World War. The top photo shows a military parade there in October 1914, while swings can be seen behind the crowds at the victory celebration in 1919.

128 The unveiling of East Barnet war memorial on 27 June 1920. It remained in the centre of the road junction until *c.*1970 when it was moved in front of the Methodist church. The latter now covers not only the site reserved for it by the board in this card but also that of the adjacent cottages.

129 Standard Telephone and Cables (STC) bought its New Southgate site in 1922, and became a major local employer. The photo of the coil and assembly shop was taken during the Second World War, when the firm's contribution to radar and other signalling was vital and 10,000 people, including for the first time many women, were employed. STC was acquired by Northern Telecom in 1990.

130 This 1923 photo shows the site of the new Edgware tube station the year before it opened. The better link made the 1867 line via Finchley uncompetitive and it was closed beyond Mill Hill East to passengers in 1939 and goods in 1964.

131 The view across from the new station colonnade to the still uncompleted Mall at Edgware in October 1926. This 'semi-Georgian' parade was developed by Leslie Raymond, one of the main local agents. It included provision for the line to pass underneath if an extension to Watford materialised.

132 The Edgware Road end of Deansbrook Lane (now Deansbrook Road) in May 1925. The familiar Cross and Raymond boards are much in evidence.

133 Change was also overtaking Hale Lane where the ford, seen here some years previously, was culverted at about this time. The Deans Brook is here the boundary between Edgware and Hendon.

134 Bourn Avenue, part of the small Conyers Park estate in New Barnet built by East Barnet UDC in the mid-1920s. The council's programme gathered pace in the 1930s but was delayed by the war. Development of the Cockfosters area in particular, though planned in the 1930s, was not completed until the 1950s.

135 Among the major arterial road schemes of the 1920s were the Edgware and Barnet Ways, part of the Watford and Barnet Bypasses. This 1927 photo shows the construction of Spur Road to link Edgware Way with Watling Street at Stanmore Corner. Another new arterial road, the M1, opened across much the same area in 1967.

Green Lane, Edgware

136 Green Lane *c.*1920. The southern section was soon suburbanised but the stretch north of Spur Road was saved by the Green Belt. In the mid-1950s this northern part was renamed Pipers Green Lane, a name earlier used only for the crescent at the southern end, now Manor Park Crescent.

137 This was the footpath between Barnet Hill and New Barnet station, before it was developed as Meadway around 1930.

138 The Lytton Road Assembly Rooms in New Barnet became a cinema in 1925, and were replaced by a purpose-built house in 1926. First the Hippodrome, then the Kinema, it became the Regal in 1933. It was converted to Bingo in 1966 and Quasar in 1993, and is seen here in 1994.

139 The still-continuing Odeon at Underhill, Barnet, in a picture taken when it opened in 1935, on the site of Underhill House.

140 The Potteries at Underhill, a common lodging-house and three cottages, may originally have been connected with a small pottery. Seen here probably in the 1930s, the group vanished in the next decade.

141a & **b** *(above left and right)* The transformation around 1930 of Church Lane into Station Road, Edgware, with only the entrance to St Margaret's church unaltered. The furthest building in the first photo is the original *Railway Hotel* built, like the station revealed in the second one, in 1867.

142 The replacement *Railway Hotel*, in 'beautiful Tudor style' and complete with gibbet inn sign, is seen here shortly after it opened in 1931. The other well-known local example of brewers' Tudor, the *Salisbury* in Barnet High Street, replaced a far earlier inn in 1929-30, and was demolished in 1988.

143 This was the view past the Ritz cinema in the year it opened, 1932. The *Edgware Gazette* claimed the cinema would 'establish Edgware as the pivotal centre of a large and increasing district' and be at night 'a beacon, blazing in magnificence across miles of country.'

144 To cater to the expanding population, Presbyterian services began in Hale Lane in 1932 and the church on the corner of Heather Walk was built in 1933. Edgware had had intermittent nonconformist congregations during the 18th and 19th centuries, a strong Congregational presence since the 1890s, and a Methodist meeting since 1924.

145 The Edgware synagogue was founded in 1930 for what was then a small congregation, and this building in Mowbray Road (now part of Rosh Pinah School and photographed in 1994) opened in 1934. The number of Jewish families grew rapidly in the 1940s and '50s, and a larger synagogue in Parnell Close was built in 1957. A Reform congregation was founded in 1935 and bought premises in Stonegrove in 1951.

146 Osidge Lane at the Pymmes Brook ford *c.*1880. A road bridge was in place by the 1890s, but otherwise this remained an ordinary country lane until it was completely suburbanised in the 1930s.

147 Russell Lane, the westward continuation of Osidge Lane, was transformed at much the same time. Here though, as this 1951 photo shows, part of the original lane was kept as a central reservation.

148 Monkfrith Way and Friars Walk, also photographed in 1951, are a typical part of the 1930s development to the north of Osidge Lane. The name Monkfrith has a local connotation (see plate 49) but Friars does not.

GALLANTS FARM ESTATE

Russell Lane, Whetstone, N.20

Which forms a compact estate, conveniently situated near London on high ground in a healthy position and which is capable of being developed with the minimum of expense.

RIPE FOR IMMEDIATE DEVELOPMENT

as a Building Estate or Sports Grounds.

45.910 Acres,

With total Frontages to Russell Lane of approx. 2,650-ft. 6-in.

THE SITUATION is unique, being the last undeveloped land within 10 miles of London. The property extends on either side of Russell Lane and is within easy reach of Railway Stations and Omnibus Services.

Arnos Grove Tube and New Southgate L.N.E.R. Main Line Stations are only 10 minutes journey by omnibus. It is only ½ a mile to Oakleigh Park Station on the L.N.E.R. Main Line.

ASPECT. The estate stands about 225 feet above sea level and has a gravelly subsoil and slopes gently towards the north-east and south-east.

THE PROPERTY consists of approx. 45.910 acres of Grass Land and includes a comfortable **FARM-HOUSE** and **HOMESTEAD** and is more particularly described later on, and is delineated on the plan attached hereto.

SERVICES are all in the immediate neighbourhood.

SEWER is laid in Russell Lane westward from Brunswick Park Road and would serve about 216-ft. Frontage of the land on the east side of the estate to the north of Russell Lane.

WATER. The main is already laid in Russell Lane for a distance of about 900 feet westwards from Brunswick Park Road and as far down as the Homestead from Oakleigh Park Road.

ELECTRICITY is only laid in Russell Lane as far down as the Houses at the Oakleigh Road end.

GAS. A gas main is laid in Russell Lane.

Any further enquiries should be made to the respective Authorities :—

The East Barnet Valley U.D.C.
The Barnet District Gas and Water Company.
The North Metropolitan Electric Power Supply Company, Ltd.
The Southgate and District Gas Company.

149 A page from the Gallants Farm sale catalogue of February 1934. Although described as Whetstone, the estate was in East Barnet. It was promptly developed and the farmhouse demolished.

150 There were some modernist developments, such as the Old Rectory Gardens Estate at Edgware, complete with suntrap windows, featured here in *Architect and Building News* for December 1933.

HOUSES AT EDGWARE

Architects : Welch, Cachemaille-Day & Lander, F. & AA.R.I.B.A.

These houses in the Old Rectory Garden Estate, built by Roger Malcolm, Ltd., have whitewashed walls and metal window frames painted green with black sills. The front doors are in green with red reveals and a surround in red brick, and the canopy over is covered with lead with a zig-zag overhang, below which the colour is green.

On the new Mill Ridge Estate in the same district, the houses are identical in elevation with these except for the use of chevron aerograph tiles round the entrance doors, and certain improvements upon the interiors of the earlier estate.

The planning is compact, simple and economical, and provides easy circulation, while the specially constructed curved windows not only provide additional light to drawing-room and principal bedroom, but lend an original appearance to the elevations. The latter are especially enhanced by the judicious use of colour in the roofing, window-frames and front doors.

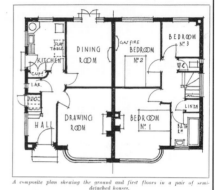

A composite plan shewing the ground and first floors in a pair of semi-detached houses.

151 John Laing's Edgware Estate was built between Edgwarebury Lane and Broadfields Avenue in 1936. This became almost the northern edge of Edgware's suburban development, and the transition thereafter from road back to rural lane is still one of the borough's surprises.

152 An early 20th-century view of the footpath from Woodside Park Finchley over the Dollis Brook and across Totteridge Fields to Laurel Farm. Today it would show Tillingham Way and Southover, which extended development from Finchley and Hendon into this corner of Totteridge in 1939. The war and then the Green Belt preserved most of the rest of Totteridge's fields.

153 Stonegrove Park a couple of years after it opened in 1934. With Edgwarebury and Deansbrook Parks, it was one of a number opened by Hendon Council around this time.

154 It was not only in newly developing areas that public parks were being opened. This was the official opening of Highland Gardens in New Barnet on 2 May 1931, when medals were presented to the East Barnet firemen.

155 In 1934, the year of this photo, Father John Ward established the Abbey Folk Museum at Hadley Hall, 89 Park Road New Barnet. The huge collection attracted many visitors but did not survive the departure of its charismatic founder *c.*1945. The house remains, in shrunken grounds, and much of the collection has since 1986 graced the Abbey Museum in Queensland, Australia.

156 MET tram: A Type H no.2224 (MET 292) tram at the Barnet terminus in 1937, the year before they were replaced by trolleybuses. The buildings behind are decorated for George VI's coronation.

WELBECK · ROAD · CELEBRATION
CORONATION OF
H · M · GEORGE VI · WEDNESDAY · 12ᵗʰ MAY · 1937

157 Beyond locating Welbeck Road in East Barnet, this splendid and ready-captioned photo needs no further gloss.

158 The change from trams to trolleybuses on the Barnet route began inauspiciously. This is a tender aiding the H1 Leyland trolleybus 756 when it broke down within yards of the terminus on the inaugural day, in March 1938.

159 A Barnet Auxiliary Fire Service team posing in 1940 outside Wellhouse Hospital (Barnet General), which housed one of the Barnet ARP (Air Raid Precautions) units.

160a & b Although less affected than inner London, this area suffered significant bombing. The top photo shows Bells Hill in 1940 and the lower one Osidge Lane in 1941.

161 East Barnet UDC adopted HMS *Musketeer* during Warship Week, March 1942, and received this commemorative photo in July 1943.

162 Swain's was another of Barnet's major photographic firms, as well as another local firm making a major contribution to the war effort. The photo-engraving factory moved to Bath Place *c.*1894, returning the plates and proofs to the London office by train. Factory and office were reunited in new Clerkenwell premises in 1970.

At Totteridge, by G.R. Smith, c.1885